I0492844

Basic Trading:

The 21 Cardinal Rules

© Copyright 2018 by Simone Capostagno - All rights reserved.

The transmission, duplication or reproduction of any of the following work including specific information will be considered an illegal act irrespective of if it is done electronically or in print. This extends to creating a secondary or tertiary copy of the work or a recorded copy and is only allowed with the express written consent from the Publisher. All additional right reserved.

The information in the following pages is broadly considered to be a truthful and accurate account of facts and as such any inattention, use or misuse of the information in question by the reader will render any resulting actions solely under their purview. There are no scenarios in which the publisher or the original author of this work can be in any fashion deemed liable for any hardship or damages that may befall them after undertaking information described herein. The author does not take any responsibility for inaccuracies, omissions, or errors which may be found therein.

Additionally, the information in the following pages is intended only for informational purposes and should thus be thought of as universal. As befitting its nature, it is presented without assurance regarding its prolonged validity or interim quality. The author of this work is not responsible for any loss, damage, or inconvenience caused as a result of reliance on information as published on, or linked to, this book.

The author of this book has taken careful measures to share vital information about the subject. May its readers acquire the right knowledge, wisdom, inspiration, and succeed.

Table of Contents

Introduction

Congratulations on downloading this book and thank you for doing so.

This book will teach you the 21 cardinal rules of trading. Regardless of the kind of trading business that you have, there are important principles or rules that you should observe. These rules can help to significantly increase your chances of success. It is important to note that knowing the rules is not enough; you also need to put them into practice to understand their real meaning.

By understanding these rules, you will be able to trade like an expert even if you are just starting out. As a beginner, you should strive to learn these rules as soon as possible. Doing so can effectively help to lower your losses and increase your profits.

You should understand that being a successful trader is not a special gift that is attainable only by a chosen few; it is something that you can learn as long as you are willing to do your best and give it enough time, dedication, and effort. With the cardinal rules in this book, you can significantly improve your chances of success and be a professional trader.

There are plenty of books on this subject on the market, so thanks again for choosing this one! Every effort was made to ensure it is full of as much useful information as possible. Please enjoy!

The 21 Cardinal Rules:

1. Buy low, sell high

This is the number one and probably the most common rule on trading: buy low, sell high. The difference between the buy price and the sell price (minus surcharges and other costs, if any) will be your profit. Although this is a fairly common rule, not all traders truly understand what it means. So, what does it mean to buy low and sell high? The only thing that you need to remember is to be able to buy something at a price that you can sell at a higher price. After all, the term *low* is relative. As long as you can sell it at a much higher price, then that is considered a *low* price. Hence, you can buy something at a high price and then sell it for profit. The important thing is to make a nice and decent profit once you sell it.

Before you buy something, you should conduct a thorough research and comparative study of the market. This is to ensure that you are getting the best deal; otherwise, you might have problems with being able to sell the asset or product at a profit.

Compare the prices of the different businesses or sellers of the product that you intend to trade. You should also contact them and try to negotiate for the best price. Most businesses will be willing to give you a discount if they notice that you are serious about the business and if they see you as a potential long-term business partner.

Now, a common mistake is to just focus on the one that gives the lowest price or offer. Although it is ideal to get the one that gives you the lowest rate, you should also consider the quality, responsiveness, degree of professionalism, and others. You would not want to work with a business that cannot keep its word or cannot deliver what it has promised. Indeed, although the rule of buying lowland selling high is mostly about the price of a product, you should also consider the overall circumstances of doing business.

It is noteworthy that this rule does not end after buying a product. Another important part of this rule is being able to sell it at a higher price to allow you to earn a decent profit. Again, your objective is to be able to sell it at a higher price than the price that you bought it for. Obviously, you should also consider the expenses and cost of doing business. If you are dealing with a volatile market like stocks or cryptocurrencies, then be sure to keep a close eye on the market.

Buying low and selling high is the hallmark for making an income in any trading business. If you are serious about being a successful trader, then be sure to master this rule.

2. Research and analysis

You should know that the life of a successful trader is full of doing research and analysis. The more that you do this, the more that you will be able to understand the market; and the more that you understand the market, the higher your chances are of making a successful trade.

It is actually the fact that you can research and analyze the market that separates the activity of trading from gambling. When you engage in trading, you should not just rely on mere luck; in a way, luck also has its part in any business. However, a key distinction is that luck does not play a major part in your success as a trader. Instead, you should rely on your own study and analysis of what is going on in the market. This will allow you to predict the direction that the market is going to take. You can then take appropriate actions to turn your knowledge into an advantage and make a profit.

It should also be noted that you are dealing with a continuously moving market, so it is only right that you do your research and analysis regularly. Indeed, the successful traders out there do not spend their time just relaxing at home. Instead, they keep a close eye on and study the market. As a trader, it is your responsibility to make sure that every trade that you make is backed up by a solid research. Remember that it is better for you not to make any trade at all, instead of entering a position when you are uncertain of the profitability of your position.

Never gamble. Unfortunately, there are many traders out there who end up gambling. It is also worth noting that doing only a little research to back up your position is not enough. Sadly, many writers on this subject fail to emphasize the importance of doing research. Just to give you an idea, even the successful and professional traders out there spend hours just to study the market. They do this on a daily basis, and yet they are still very careful whenever they enter a trading position. This is only to emphasize the importance of doing research. It is a very common mistake to do insufficient research. Again, it is better for you not to make any trade at all instead of entering a trade that you have not thoroughly research and analyzed. Know that the life of a trader is full of trials and errors. This is why you should conduct research and analysis continuously.

Be sure that you gather only high-quality information. Keep in mind that your analysis will depend on the information that you have. Hence, if the information that you have is wrong, then you cannot expect to come up with a sound trading decision.

There are different ways to analyze data. As a trader, there are two important strategies that you should know: fundamental analysis and technical analysis.

So, what is fundamental analysis? It is also called as the *lifeblood of investment*. By the name given to it, it is obvious that it is considered very important. Fundamental analysis deals with the basics; hence, it is about the fundamentals. After all, if you do not understand the basics, then it is impossible for you to come up with a sound trading decision. When you use fundamental analysis, you should know and analyze the different factors that can influence the price of the product, commodity, asset, or item that you are selling. Hence, be sure to be updated on the news. You should also pay attention to the economy, as well as any developments or changes in the market and technology. You should also consider market behavior and acceptance, among others. This analysis is probably the one that demands the most time and effort, but it is also very effective. Also, do not think that just because you have researched the market for several hours today means that you are in the best position to make a sound investment decision. You should know that professional and successful traders out there apply fundamental analysis for hours on a daily basis. Keep in mind that if you are not completely confident of your position, then do not make any trades. Instead, focus on doing more research. You are probably familiar with the saying: "Knowledge is power." This is what fundamental analysis is about. But, of course, knowledge is only good if you make use of it. The more knowledge that you have and analyze, the more likely that you can come up with the right investment decision.

Now that you know what fundamental analysis is, it is time to discuss technical analysis. If you are more of a visual person, then you will probably like this approach. Technical analysis makes use of graphs and charts to study the price movements of the asset or item that you are trading. By analyzing the price behavior of an asset, you will be able to determine the direction that it will take on the market. The idea behind this approach is that all of the factors that affect the price of an asset have their final effect on the price. Therefore, by simply analyzing the price movements, you also get to deal with all the said factors. It can be said that technical analysis is the simplified version of fundamental analysis. Instead of reading lots of information, you simply have to analyze a particular graph or chart.

When you use technical analysis, you should learn to read patterns. Okay, you might be wondering if patterns exist. The answer is *yes*. However, you should be careful since patterns come and go. This means that you should not expect to always see a pattern. Just because you have spent several hours looking at a graph does not mean that there is a pattern for you to see. A common mistake is to force yourself to see a pattern even when no pattern exists. Be patient and always exercise an unbiased and open mind.

Many experts say that technical analysis is a good strategy to use for short-term trades, while fundamental analysis is more suitable for long-term trading positions. It is also noteworthy that both strategies can be combined with other trading strategies. In fact, many successful traders rely on using both fundamental and technical analysis at the same time. When you engage in trading, remember that the more effort that you put into your research and analysis, the more likely that you will be able to make the right trading decision.

3. Use proper timing

Timing is essential in business. This is true especially when you are engaged in a trading business. You should learn to ride and play along with the volatility of the market. The market you are dealing with may be more volatile than you think. Many times, instead of facing a difficult market, the best and most practical thing to do would be to just wait it out. Be patient and learn to wait out the bad times in the market. It is common for the market to have its highs and lows. The important thing is to be there when the market is a bull market. A bull market is a situation in the market that signifies that the prices are increasing or are about to increase. This is the best time to enter the market and make a trade. Trading does not have to be difficult. If you spend enough time in the market, you will notice that there are times when it is easy to make a profit. You do not need to give yourself a hard time. If you learn to identify such opportunities when they come, then you can make trades only during such times. After all, no one is forcing you to make a trade, so just do it when you know that you have the upper hand.

Knowing the best timing to enter and exit a trading position can be tricky. There are no hard and fast rules on how to go about doing it. Indeed, learning to observe proper timing requires practice. This is something that you will learn through experience. A piece of advice: learn to identify when the market is a bear market or a bull market. As we have mentioned, a bull market describes a market where the prices are increasing or are about to increase, while a bear market describes a market where the prices are falling or are about to fall. If you are able to recognize when it is a bear or a bull market, then you can use that knowledge to your advantage and make a nice profit.

An important part of learning how to observe proper timing is to realize that sometimes the best thing to do is to not take any action. Yes, there are times when the best option is simply to observe the market and wait for a much better opportunity to profit. A common mistake committed by beginners is to make trades every time that they are able to. Of course, professional and expert traders know better. They know that they should only make a trade when they are confident of their position. Hence, there are times that you just have to wait for a better opportunity. Needless to say, when that opportunity comes, then be sure to grab it and take advantage of it. Indeed, learning to observe proper timing is an essential skill that you need to be successful at.

One thing that defeats proper timing is being impatient. This means being impatient while waiting for the best opportunity to commence a trade. Take note that just because you have some money in your trading account does not mean that you should open a trade. Experts know that one should only assume a trading position if he is confident of his position. Be patient and wait for your turn to hit a nice profit. If your confidence level is less than 60%, then it is suggested that you just observe the market and wait for a better opportunity. Accept the fact that it is now a part of your regular routine to conduct research and analysis. Just because you have studied a particular set of information for hours, does not mean that you should commence a trade. That is not how it works when you work as a trader. The life of a trader is full of trials and errors. Make sure that you closely study the market and be there when an opportunity arises.

4. Keep it simple

Trading should not be complicated. If you think of it as something complicated, then chances are you probably do not understand it properly. Avoid strategies that make the activity of trading appear too complicated. A simple and direct approach is recommended. However, just because it is simple does not mean that you do not need to exert time and effort. In fact, if you are serious about becoming a successful trader, then you should know that you need to be committed to it. A simple approach would mean doing research and continuous analysis of the market. This, of course, takes time. Hence, even though you take a simple approach, know that it still involves doing work.

Although simple, the activities of a trader take a lot of work. Being a trader is already hard as it is, so do not make it complicated. If you come to think about it, trading is actually a straightforward approach; you simply have to ensure that you are able to sell what you have at a higher price than when you bought it.

A common mistake is to make it complicated in order to justify to yourself that you are doing something important. Take note that what matters in a trade is if you are able to make a profit from it. It is not the method that you use or the level of complications. Keep it simple and always do your best.

There is power in simplicity. In fact, many of the effective strategies out there are simple enough. Take, for example, fundamental analysis. As a responsible trader, it is only right that you examine the basics or the fundamentals before you make a trading decision. Any responsible person would want to see and understand the basic element that can influence a trade. As you can see, there is no magic here. The approach is simple and straightforward. Some say that the simplicity of an approach is what makes it effective. If something still appears complicated to you, it is often a sign that you do not understand it completely, so it is a good idea to take a closer look. When you work as a trader, you should ensure that you have a good and correct understanding of what is happening in the market that you participate in. This is a basic requirement. After all, if you do not know your market, then it would be hard, if not impossible, for you to come up with a sound trading decision.

5. Consider mass psychology

Although understanding the economy is important, you should also pay attention to mass or market psychology. You should consider how the market reacts to changes. Take note that the economy is not the only factor that affects the prices of assets, products, or items. You should learn to understand mass psychology and be able to predict how the people will respond. If you are able to do this, then you will be able to identify the best course of action to take.

When you consider mass psychology, you should also take into consideration how the people feel. Indeed, emotions play a major role in the market. As a professional trader, it is true that you are trained to not allow yourself to be controlled by emotions. However, the fact is that the majority of traders are led by their emotions, and you need to keep this fact under consideration. Hence, you should also consider it every time you make a trading decision. How the market responds will definitely have a strong impact on the direction that the market will take. After all, no matter how the economy is doing, and despite its current state, the final say, whether you will make a profit or not will primarily depend upon the market. Take note that the market is composed of people, and many of these people are very much influenced by their emotions.

One thing that you should remember is that it is the nature of the market to change. Hence, do not expect for it to take the same position over time. Instead, know and expect that it will change sooner or later, just as the preferences of the people also change over time.

When you analyze the market, you should try to see things from the perspective of the people. A common mistake is to be narcissistic and become too centered on what you think, instead of considering what many other people think. It is noteworthy that the direction of the market is highly influenced by how other traders respond.

Take note that this does not just refer to any simple psychology. Instead, it talks about mass psychology, which teaches you to focus on a big part of the market. You should consider how the different factors that affect the prices of assets, also affect market behavior. If you are able to identify the market behavior that is applicable, then you can easily take steps to take advantage of it.

Understanding mass psychology is not that hard. In fact, by simply watching or reading related news, you can somehow gauge how the market will respond. For example, some time ago, when China declared that it would shut down all of its cryptocurrency exchanges, the price of bitcoin and many altcoins dropped. However, when Russia declared that it would no longer outlaw the use of cryptocurrencies in its territory, the price of bitcoin increased. As you can see, certain changes in the market affect market behavior. If it is good news, then positive market behavior can be expected. Of course, the opposite can be expected in case the contrary happens.

Learning to read mass psychology is an important skill that you should develop. It is something that you will find extremely useful in your journey as a trader. It should be noted that the whole market economy is driven primarily by people. Hence, if you are able to understand how these people think and feel, then you are already one step ahead.

Although mass psychology is something that is considered important, you should be careful with allowing it to direct your actions. When the market is in panic, people usually end up making the wrong decisions. Hence, even though you are aware that the market is in a panic, it does not mean that you also have to be affected and panic as well. Instead, you should stay calm and use your knowledge to your advantage by taking more appropriate actions.

6. Learn from your mistakes

No matter how careful you are, you will surely commit a mistake along the way. In fact, you should expect to commit mistakes from time to time. This is also how you will learn. Instead of feeling so bad and blaming yourself, you should relax and learn from every mistake. This does not mean that you should allow yourself to commit mistakes, rather, you should always do your best. However, if you still commit mistakes, then make the best of it by learning from the experience instead of feeling down and disappointed. Take as much time as you need to reflect on and learn from a mistake so that you will not commit the same or similar mistakes.

Success is about doing the right things and avoiding, or at least minimizing your mistakes. Indeed, regardless of how careful you are, you can expect to encounter some losses along the way. Do not worry; this is normal. What is important is to be in a positive profit once you add up everything. Do not let a mistake go unnoticed. You have to learn from it. This is how you shape and train yourself to be a better trader.

Every professional and successful trader has his share of mistakes. No matter how careful you approach the market, you will surely commit some mistakes one way or another. This is part of the learning process. With every mistake that you encounter along the way, you should give yourself time to reflect on it. A mistake is only a mistake if you do not learn anything from it; otherwise, you may consider it as a lesson that will help you become a better trader. The more you improve, the more you can pave your way to success.

7. Be open to change

You should also realize that you are dealing with a continuously moving and evolving market. As such, you should be open to change. You cannot expect for the market to remain consistent or stagnant. Just as people and businesses change, so does the market that you are engaged in. This also means that you should be able to adapt quickly. You should also remember that the more volatile the market is, the quicker it changes. Of course, change can be good or bad, depending on the circumstances. Now, just because the market changes and is headed towards a positive direction, does not mean that you should relax and lower your guard. The life of a trader is an active one. Keep in mind that change is in the nature of the market. Hence, you cannot afford to be overconfident and just trust in the market. There are so many things that can happen in the course of a trade, and there are so many factors that can affect your position. Hence, be ready for an adverse change and prepare for it. The best way to do this is to keep your eye on the market. Just as the market can change, you should also learn to change your position when necessary.

You should also learn to be flexible. Trading is about taking the right positions at the right time. Of course, this is easier said than done. To be ready, then expect for change and be ready when it happens. Regardless of what market that you engage in, know that it is always subject to change. This is because, the market is made of people who have their own preferences and biases; and last but not least, people change. Take note that change is not a bad thing. In fact, it is what allows you to make a nice profit. The important thing is to learn to be in the right position when the market changes.

Change is a relative term. It may also refer to negative changes in the market. As such, you have to be flexible enough to adapt and adjust to market changes. There are also changes that can occur without any warning. This is part of the risk of engaging in a real market environment. As a trader, you should learn how to deal with these changes, whether good or bad. To be open to change also means being ready for it when it happens. This is why you should have a contingency plan, as well as other plans in place. This is to better prepare yourself for anything that can happen along the course of a trade. Of course, it is impossible to be able to prepare for all types of contingencies, but at least be ready for those that are foreseeable. There is no other way to do this but to study the market regularly.

8. Do not be greedy

Greed has caused many traders to lose their money. It is a basic rule in trading that you should not be greedy. Unfortunately, even those who are already well aware of this rule still fall for it. So, how do you know when you are being greedy, and how can you avoid it? Many people only realize that they have been greedy when it is too late — after losing their money. Greed happens when you intend to take more than what your position deserves. A good example of greed is continuously holding on to a profitable position until the market changes and the price of the asset drops. The undesirable consequences of greed usually have a good beginning. Indeed, many traders do not lose their money for failing to identify the right assets to invest in. Instead, they pick the right assets but hold on to them for too long. You should keep in mind that every market has its share of volatility. If you get greedy, then the market will soon turn against your favor. This is why exiting a trading position is just as important as entering one.

So, how can you avoid greed? Well, the best way to do this is to have a plan and to stick to that plan. Indeed, greed can be more tempting than you might think. Once you are already in the game, you might not even notice how it operates until it is too late. The best way to know if you are being greedy is to ensure that you are sticking to your plan. Any moment that you feel like deviating away from that plan, especially if the reason is to earn more profit, then chances are you are on your way to being greedy.

Being greedy is not always a bad thing. If it works, then you can, indeed, earn money. However, you cannot expect to be in a positive profit in the long run if you continue to be greedy. This is because, when you allow yourself to be greedy, you also tend to take a more aggressive approach where you expose yourself to more risks. Although this presents an opportunity for you to profit, it also exposes you to a level of risk that is likely more than what your trading position can handle. What is more, a single mistake can often lead to losing all of your money.

Especially if you are just starting out as a trader, it is important for you to take a conservative approach. In fact, it is recommended that you take advantage of the demo account that is provided by your broker (if any). If not, then it is advised that you start out small. As a beginner, you should understand that your objective is not to make money right away, but to be familiar with the actual trading experience in a live market.

You should always keep your greed under control. Although the reason you engage in trading is to make money, too much greed will only cause you to lose all of your money.

Another way to prevent yourself from being greedy is to focus on increasing your rate of success, instead of the amount of money that you earn per trade. After all, if you can increase your rate of success (successful trades vs. losing trades), then you will most likely end up with a positive profit. The moment you feel that greed is overcoming you, stop whatever it is that you are doing and never make a new trade. You should examine the situation with a clear mind. Remember to be objective in your approach. It is better for you to have earned just a little profit, instead of taking so much risk and relying on luck just to earn a big amount. Again, as a professional trader, you should know well that you must not rely on luck. Last but not least, you must never be greedy. You can continue to enjoy a smooth and continuous flow of profits as long as you do your job properly as a trader.

9. Write a trading journal

This is not really a requirement, yet many professional traders strongly recommend that you do this: write a trading journal. This is a good way for you to view yourself from a different perspective — from a standpoint that is free from any bias and prejudice. Do not worry; you do not need to be a professional writer to keep a trading journal. There are only two things that you need to remember: you should update your trading journal regularly, and you should be honest with everything that you write in your journal.

Since it is your own journal, you are free to write anything that you want that is related to trading. Ideally, your journal should include your reasons for trading, your goals and objectives, your plans and strategies, and your current open trades, among others.

In the first few weeks, you might not appreciate the value of having a journal. However, just persist in writing in it. After some time, you will start to appreciate its value, especially when you begin to notice your progress. It should also be noted that a trading journal is not just a notebook where you write down your thoughts and experiences; it is not just about writing. More importantly, the purpose of a trading journal is to allow you to make reflections. Hence, make it a habit to read your journal every now and then and make reflections. Indeed, there are lessons that you can learn from your journal that you would otherwise overlook. This is the value of having a trading journal.

Now, there are people who do not write their journal simply because they are not fond of the actual writing activity. The thing is, you do not need to write in a notebook. If you want to, you can simply have a file on your computer or you can even use a mobile application. Mobile phones these days have a writing application that you can use to write down your thoughts. Just be sure not to lose your file. The important thing is for you to have something to write on and be able to track your progress.

When writing a journal, honesty is very important. If you are not honest with your records, then you will have a hard time being able to estimate your position. A common mistake is not accepting one's mistakes or weaknesses. Take note that this is an important part and is crucial to your success. In fact, the more weaknesses that you can write down, the better it will be for you.

The keys to an effective trading journal are honesty and consistency. Be consistent and update your journal regularly. It should act like a mirror that reflects your position in the market as a trader. It is hard to appreciate the value of a journal if you just read about it. The best way to know if this is for you is to give it a try. Try to give it at least three months before you drop the idea of using a journal. Indeed, there are many lessons that you can learn from your trading journal.

10. Learn from others

When you work as a trader, you undergo a process of continuous learning. One of the best ways to learn is by learning from other people. Do not just learn from their successes, but also learn from their mistakes. Today, it is very easy to connect with people and learn. There are many groups and forums that you can join online. There are also many traders who write blogs, articles, and books on the subject. Just remember to always take their words with a grain of salt. Still, by exposing yourself to others, you will surely find interesting ideas and viewpoints that can help you grow as a trader. Continuous improvement involves continuously learning from other people. Do not just read or know what happened to them. A good way to learn is to put yourself in their situation. Would you have acted the same way? Try to analyze their story from their own perspective.

Just a word of caution: It is fairly easy to promote a person as an expert if properly marketed, especially if you use the power of social media. Hence, do not believe every person who claims to be an expert right away. Instead, check and test their ideas in the real market. Sadly, there are "experts" out there who have more losses than profits.

It is also a good idea if you can meet with other traders in person. Sharing is learning, so there are definitely a lot of things that you can learn from other people. Also, do not hesitate to share what you know with others, including your experiences. Try to form a mutual bond of friendship with other traders. After all, you are not competing against one another. This is one of the best things about being a trader; you do not have to worry so much about competition. Of course, this will still depend on the kind of trading business that you have.

It is not unusual to commit the mistakes that you are already aware of. There simply are mistakes that are difficult to avoid. If ever this happens to you, do not get discouraged. Instead, learn from the experience and move on. Again, the life of a trader is a continuous process of learning. If you persist, then you will soon commit less or no mistakes, and enjoy a constant flow of profits. Now, keep in mind that just as you learn from the experiences and mistakes of others, you should also share what you know and let other people learn from you.

Depending on the specific market that you participate in, you will definitely find related groups online. Although not a requirement, you will most likely find it helpful to join such groups and meet like-minded people who have the same interest. Not to mention, learning how other traders think is also a good way to predict the direction that the market is going to take. After all, the traders themselves, how they buy and sell assets and others, have an effect on the price movements of an underlying asset, item, or commodity.

Pay attention to other traders, especially to the mistakes that they have committed. As much as possible, try to avoid committing the same mistakes. Another important thing to take note of is to find out what they did after a particular mistake. If you think that they dealt with the mistake the right way, then you will know how to deal with the same problem if ever you fall into the same pitfall. As you can see, learning from mistakes is not just a matter of avoiding problems, but it is also a way to prepare you if ever the problem arises. This is the essence of learning; it makes you a better trader.

11. Diversify

You are probably familiar with the saying that you should not put all your eggs in one basket. This is what diversifying is about. When you engage in a trading business, you should not put all of your investments in a single trade. In other words, do not go all in. Instead, you should diversify by spreading your positions. By doing so, you are able to spread your risks. Just imagine what will happen if you put everything you have, into one trade that ends up going under. You will lose a substantial amount of your invested capital. To avoid this, you can make multiple trades, instead of having a single trading position.

Now, a common mistake that people make when they diversify is to take their trading positions for granted. They think that since they are going to open many positions, then they can afford to lose some of those trading positions. Although this is true and is, in fact, the essence of diversifying, it does not mean that you should take any trading position for granted. Do not convince yourself that since you have multiple positions, that it is now okay for you to lose some trades. As much as possible, always strive to keep all your positions profitable. Remember that it is better for you not to trade at all, rather than take any trade for granted.

Diversifying necessarily includes more work. This is because you will deal with having multiple trades. Make sure that every trade that you make is backed up by solid research. Diversifying is not an excuse for you to be lazy. It is a way for you to spread your risks in an attempt to minimize your losses.

When you diversify, it means that you will have to do more research. Indeed, this is probably why there are some traders who do not like to diversify their positions. However, you need to accept this in order to spread your risks. After all, you should keep in mind that, there is no amount of research or any other kind of preparation that can guarantee the success of a trade. No matter how profitable a certain position is, there is always the possibility that it might change. Once again, the market is always subject to change.

It is up to you how much you are willing to diversify. You can diversify by trading other assets in the same industry, but it can also be as far as trading assets that belong to a completely different industry. This is a matter of your personal preferences. There is really no strict rule as to how you should diversify. The important thing is that it should allow you to effectively lower your potential losses and help you earn profits. Just be sure that when you diversify, you should have a competent knowledge of whatever it may be that you diversify to. After all, even if you diversify, if you fail to make those trades work, then you will also encounter a bad loss. Hence, to stay in profit, you should ensure that every trade position that you have is likely to be profitable. Of course, this will require diligent and continuous research and analysis on your part.

If you know different strategies, you can also use them to diversify your positions. The best strategy to use in the market also changes depending on the situation. This is why it is a good idea to learn as many strategies as possible. Take note also that learning means more than reading the strategies. You also need to practice them in a real market situation. Now, when you diversify, just be sure to use effective strategies that can significantly increase your chances of making a profit.

12. Have a plan

As a trader, it is important that you always have a plan. You should have a short-term plan and a long-term plan. You should also have a contingency plan. This is to prepare you for anything that can happen in the market. Keep in mind that the market has its share of volatility. It can change even without due notice. To be ready for all forms of contingencies, you should always have a plan. In order to avoid being greedy, be sure to have a short-term plan. This is important, especially if you are just starting out. For example, let us say that for a particular trade, you plan to profit by 10%. If you hit that 10% target, then exercise the discipline to exit the position. If you are still a beginner, it is best to always stick to your plan as you learn to be more familiar with how the market works. Having a long-term plan is also essential to always give you a sense of direction. There are simply so many things that can happen in the market. If you do not have a plan, then it can be easy for you to get lost. You should also have a contingency plan. A contingency plan is what you will do in case the worst possible situation happens in the market. Although the chances for it to happen are slim, it is best to be ready if it should occur. Having a contingency plan is important. In the course of your life being a trader, there will come a time when you will definitely make use of a contingency plan. This can help to effectively minimize your losses.

Having a plan is one thing, executing it is another. As a trader, you should learn to execute your plan properly and effectively. Take note that planning is not just about setting your goals and objectives; it also includes identifying the right actions to achieve them. Once you have a plan, needless to say, you have to stick to it. Now, there are instances when a trader should stray away from his plan. This will depend on the situation. However, there are two conditions that you should meet before you abandon a plan. The first condition is that you should thoroughly study the alternative action to be taken; otherwise, it might even be worse than your original plan. The second condition is that the alternative action should be better than your previous plan. This means that it should allow you to profit more, or at least help to minimize your potential losses. Generally, plans are not something that you just abandon easily; just as it takes time and effort to come up with a good plan. Having a plan gives you an outline or at least a skeleton of what you should do. Hence, it is important that you exercise diligence and care in coming up with a plan.

It is also noteworthy that a plan is something that you should make before you even start to make a move. Unfortunately, there are those who commit the mistake of coming up with a plan only while they are already in the middle of a trade. By this time, it will already be too late for you to set up a good plan, as you will be dictated by the market environment. Hence, to come up with a more effective plan, you should do it before you even commence any trade.

13. Have a professional approach

You should always observe a professional approach. Many people consider trading as a hobby. Although there is really nothing wrong with this, you should not expect too much if you only consider trading as a mere hobby. When you engage in trading, you will usually get what you deserve. Most of the time, whether you make a profit or not will depend on the time and effort that you put into a trade. If you give it more research and study, then chances are you will most likely come up with the right trading decision. However, if you just consider it as a hobby and only do a quick research on the subject, then you should not expect to make a substantial profit from it. Just to give you an idea, professional and highly successful traders spend hours on a daily basis just analyzing the market, and yet, they are still very careful whenever they enter or exit a trading position.

It is true that many people start out trading as a hobby. Just remember that if you take the same approach, then you should not expect to earn so much profit from it. Just the fact that you only take it as a hobby, signifies lack of commitment and dedication. If you know that you cannot give it enough time, then it is suggested that you just trade part-time instead of trading full-time as a hobby. The important thing is to take a professional approach and emphasize the importance of commitment and hard work.

Taking a professional approach means much more than affirming that you are taking what you do seriously. It also requires positive actions on your part. If you are already busy with your work, then just be a professional part-time trader. This will allow you to make a few trades, but still ensure the quality of your trading positions. However, if you can, it is still advisable that you try to be a full-time trader. If you cannot quit your day job, then you can start as a part-time trader. When you think that you are ready to leave the regular nine-to-five office job, then you can shift into trading full-time. This will depend on your personal situation. If you think that you can afford to take risks, and if you have enough money, then trading full-time can be a lot of fun. There are people who trade full-time and are happy with their decision. If you ever intend to take this path, then just be ready to render some serious work, especially in terms of research and analysis. Although trading can be done in the comfort of your home, it is not as easy as it seems. If you slack on doing your research, then you risk losing a trade, which means losing your money. When you work as a trader, you are responsible for everything. Even though you are your own boss, there is also no one else for you to depend on but yourself.

If you are not yet ready to take a professional approach, then it is advised that you should only trade using small amounts of money. If you are not ready to give it enough time and effort, then do not expect to earn a high amount of profit. Hence, only use small amounts to minimize your risks and losses.

14 Cash out

There are still traders out there who are simply stubborn enough to not withdraw their profits. Instead, they continue to invest in new open trading positions. The idea is to increase the funds in order to increase the potential profit. If you come to think of it, this is not a bad idea at all. After all, if you want to earn a bigger profit, then you should trade using bigger funds. However, what some traders do not realize is that withdrawing your profits is also very important. If you just keep your profits in your account, then it's as if you were merely using a demo account. You need to understand that the only way to fully realize your profit, is when you are able to turn it into cash. The only way to do this is by making a withdrawal. Don't worry, you do not need to withdraw all of your funds or profits right away. If you want, you can just withdraw just 20% of your profits. The important thing is to make a withdrawal every now and then. Not only will this allow you to enjoy your profits, but it is also an effective way to minimize your risks and potential losses. Take note that, as long as you keep your funds in your account, they remain exposed to risks. The only way to save them and not risking anything is by making a withdrawal. Again, you do not need to withdraw all of your funds right away. It is, of course, a good idea to try to grow the funds in your trading account. Just be sure that you also make a withdrawal. There are no hard and fast rules as to how much you should withdraw. This book suggests that you withdraw at least 15% of your profits if any. Of course, you will only cash out if you make a nice profit. In case of a loss, then there is probably no good reason for you to make a withdrawal, except if you want to stop trading altogether.

Cashing out is easy if you trade online. Thanks to technology, there are many things that you can trade just by going online. This is a good way to manage your own trading business in the comfort of your home. With the use of technology, you can now trade different assets like stocks, cryptocurrencies, foreign currencies, and others, completely online with just a few clicks of the mouse.

You are also free to adjust the amount or rate that you will withdraw. If you want to put more priority in increasing your funds, then you might want to withdraw at a lower rate. Again, there is no strict rule on this matter. Feel free to exercise your own preference depending on the strategy that you are using. If you are using an aggressive strategy, then it is advised that you make a bigger withdrawal to compensate for the aggressiveness of the strategy. Still, this is a matter that is up to you to decide. The important thing is to ensure to make a reasonable amount of withdrawals.

15. Do not chase after your losses

This advice is normally given to gamblers. However, the same advice also applies when you are engaged in a trading business. Now, the surprising truth is that many of those people who commit this mistake are the ones who are well aware that they should not chase after their losses. This means that they know this rule, yet they still violate it. So, how does this happen? Well, the truth is that it's very easy to plunge into this pitfall, which explains why even those who are aware of it still commit the same mistake. This usually occurs after a bad loss. The tendency is to try to do everything that you can to recover your losses, and this may include taking an aggressive approach. However, the problem here is that you will most likely end up with more losses. Take note that this approach does not mean that you will always lose your money. In fact, if you get lucky, you might be able to recover all of your losses and even earn some profits. However, the risk is just too high that your funds and strategy may not be ready for it. Although it can allow you to make money, you cannot expect to be in a positive profit in the long run if you continue to chase after your losses, due to its high risk.

Instead of chasing after your losses, the recommended approach is to chase after more profits. If you encounter a loss, then accept it as it happens. Do not chase after it. Doing so will only increase your risks. In the course of your life as a trader, it is inevitable that you will encounter some losses along the way. This is true no matter how much research and preparation that you do. There are simply so many things that can happen in the course of a trade. But, do not be discouraged. The important thing is to be in a positive profit when you add up everything (profits and losses).

Chasing after your losses compels you to take an aggressive approach. The problem here is that your strategy and funds may not be ready for it. Hence, whenever you feel that you are being tempted to chase after your losses, the best thing that you should do is to stop and calm down. Instead of thinking about the loss, you should think positive and focus on earning more profits. After all, in the end, the important thing is how much profit you have made, if any. Always take a positive approach. Focusing on your losses will only give you a negative mindset.

Take note that there are certain strategies that will seem as if you are chasing after your losses, although that is not exactly the case. If used in a strategy, then such aggressiveness is also used strategically. Take note, however, that if you are just starting out, then it is strongly advised that you stay away from any kind of aggressive strategy. Just to give you an idea of what is ideal, especially for beginners, many experts suggest that you should not trade more than 5% of your total funds per position.

16 Do not be an emotional trader

Although it is good to have passion in what you do, it is not right to be an emotional trader. You should never allow your emotions to cloud your judgement and rational thinking. When you engage in trading, you must always take an objective approach. This is the kind of job where you are absolutely on your own. The market does not care if you profit or not. It does not even know you, and it will continue to function regardless of what happens to your trades. You can say that being a trader is like being in a harsh environment. Just as you are your own boss, you are also absolutely responsible for everything. As a professional trader, you should always be objective at all times. If you ever notice that you are being influenced by your emotions, then you should stop and calm down. You cannot come up with an intelligent decision if you are controlled by your emotions. Hence, as a professional trader, you should keep your emotions in check at all times. Never allow your feelings or emotions to dictate the direction of your trade. Every action or trade that you do should always be backed up by solid research and analysis. If a trade is supported by nothing more than a mere hunch, then it is better if you do not enter that trade. Remember to be objective at all times. You are responsible for everything.

This is easier said than done. In the cures of a trade, especially once you are already invested in it, it can easily be swept away by your emotions. Once you have invested your time, money, and efforts into this venture, then it becomes easy to be influenced by your emotions. However, this is not an excuse. As a professional, you should not allow your emotions to cloud your way of thinking. Be objective and reasonable at all times and use your emotions to your advantage.

17. Continuous practice and improvement

As a trader, you should know the importance of continuous practice and improvement. There is simply no end to learning and development. It is also with noting that the rules in this book are not just meant to be read. The only way to fully understand what these rules mean is by applying them. Hence, you have to put them into actual practice.

As a professional trader, you should know that there is no end to development. Just as the market continues to evolve, so should you, continuing to develop your winning strategy. Do not be discouraged, even if you fail to observe these rules in the first few weeks of trading. You should understand that learning to trade effectively is like learning a new skill. As such, you should already expect that it will take time and practice. It is important that you do not stop practicing. Do not underestimate the market that you are dealing with, and make sure that your strategy is flexible enough to adapt to sudden market changes.

True professional traders are never satisfied with what they know. They always seek ways to improve. You should also strive to do the same if you want to be a successful trader. Always keep in mind that there is no end to development.

It is also not enough to just know a strategy; you should strive for mastery. Traders know just how challenging it is to deal with a living and evolving market, so it is only right to always do your best and keep an eye for further improvements. Continuous improvement is only possible through positive actions. To practice trading is to actually engage in the activity of trading. Always remember that the more that you practice, the more that you can also improve as a trader.

18. Use a stop-loss limit

This is a rule that will help you to effectively minimize your potential losses. This is a must, especially when you use an aggressive strategy. Having a stop-loss limit will prevent you from risking beyond what you are willing to risk in a trade. This way, you can assure that you will not lose all of your funds, even if a particular trade does not end favorably. So, how do you use a stop-loss limit? You should set a certain limit *before* you even enter a trade. For example, you can decide that you are only willing to risk up to 10% of your funds in a trade. Assuming that you are using an aggressive strategy where you increase the amount being traded, then you should stop once you reach your set limitation. This is why it is called a *stop-loss limit*. It is the certain limit where you will stop chasing after your losses or increasing the wager in a trade. Needless to say, an important part of this rule is to observe your limit if you ever reach it. Simply accept whatever loss you might suffer and move on. Once again, you should not focus on chasing after your losses. Instead, keep your focus on chasing after more profits. The purpose of this strategy is to prevent you from risking beyond what you are willing or able to risk. Just be sure to respect the limitation that you set.

19. Never underestimate the volatility of the market

Every market has its own share of volatility. There are markets that have high volatility, and there are also those that have low volatility. It is also not uncommon for a market to shift from a low-volatility market into a high-volatility market, and vice versa. What is volatility? The term "volatility" refers to how an asset or an item changes its price in the market over time. A market with a high volatility means that the prices of the assets in that market can change quickly within a short period of time. A market with a low volatility describes a market where the prices of the assets do not change quickly. Regardless of the kind of market that you are dealing with, you should pay attention to how the market moves, and especially how it changes. Volatility is not a bad thing. In fact, it is the volatility of the market that allows you to earn a profit.

A common mistake is to get too careless after winning a few trades. You should understand that every trade is different from all the others. Hence, just because you have made a series of successful trades, it does not guarantee that your next trade will also be as successful. It will primarily depend on the amount and quality of research and analysis that you do.

When it comes to volatility, the rule is that, the higher the volatility is, the higher the potential profit will be. Keep in mind that volatility refers to changes in the price. However, it should also be noted that, the higher the volatility is, the higher the risk will also be. Just as you could profit by a high amount in a market that is highly volatile, there is also the risk that you lose quickly. Hence, you should always be careful with every trading position that you make. In order to increase your chances of success, be sure to do your homework and conduct diligent research and analysis of the market.

To be able to follow the market movement, it is advised that you follow closely on the latest and related news. You should conduct your own research of the market, and also pay attention to the level of competition, as well as market acceptance. The more quality information that you can gather, the better.

Depending on how you are positioned, the volatility of the market can be either good or bad. Hence, you need to keep your eye on it. Know that the market trend can and will change. As a trader, you should train yourself to be ready for all kinds of situations in the market. If you are just starting out, then it can be quite a challenge. However, as you gain more experience and wisdom, you will soon be able to deal with the changing market more effectively.

20. Do not focus on the money

A common approach that beginners do is to focus primarily on the money. After all, the reason why you trade is to earn a profit, right? Hence, it is only logical that you focus on the money. Although this may seem correct, expert traders know better. They know that by focusing on the money or profit that you can potentially earn does not give you an edge against the market. Instead of spending their energy focusing too much on how much money they can earn, they focus on the actions or the things that they have to do to earn a profit. This, of course, requires positive actions, like doing research or making computations instead of just daydreaming of the profits that you can earn. Expert traders know that money or profits will come as long as you trade properly. Hence, instead of being divided and focusing too much on the money, you should instead focus on what needs to be done to earn a nice profit. As long as you trade strategically and responsibly, then chances are that you will earn a nice profit.

In casino gambling, there is saying that goes like this: "Money is only there to keep you in the game." Money should not be your main focus. Rather, it should be more about beating the system with your strategy, and through diligent research and analysis. If you do well, then the money will follow.

The more you grow as a trader, the more you will understand that money is just a part of the activities of being a professional trader. After all, you do not earn a profit just by thinking about money. Instead, you have to deal with, and analyze the actual market situation. Money will soon become like a mere reward every time you do an excellent job.

21. Have a trader's mindset

Having a trader's mindset is important to your success. As the saying goes, "It's all in the mind." If you have the right mindset that is fit for trading, then you will most likely succeed. The right mindset for trading is one that is objective and applies the strategies effectively. The mind should not succumb to greed but remain focused on how the market moves. All the rules in this book should already be second nature to you.

Just as you should not submit to greed, you should also not succumb to fear. Fear is when you are too afraid to risk anything, potentially missing out on opportunities. An important part of trading is applying the right strategies. Although strategies are not a part of the coverage of this book (except fundamental and technical analysis), it is important to note that you should not commence any trade without applying any effective strategy.

The right trader's mindset should not panic, regardless of what happens in the market. You should understand that both winning and losing are a natural part of the life of being a trader. The important thing is to be in a positive profit once you add up everything.

The ideal trader's mindset should cling to doing research and analysis. Indeed, as a professional trader, research and analysis shall be the foundation of your success. The more that you know and understand the market, the more that you will be able to come up with the right trading decisions.

A true trader also does not depend on other people but instead has his own view and understanding of the market. Even as a beginner, it is your job to form your own estimate or view of the market. Do not forget that even the true experts out there also commit mistakes, and they also share conflicting views.

The right trader's mindset only takes calculated risks. Keep in mind that you are not gambling. Hence, you are not obliged to make or assume a trade if you are not confident of your position.

It is noteworthy that having the right trader's mindset normally takes time to achieve. It is the mindset that is most ideal for trading. It is always open to new learnings and opportunities without being too aggressive. Do not worry if you think that you still have not attained this kind of mindset. The important thing is to keep on practicing and developing. If you train yourself well, then you can soon be a very successful trader and pave your own path to financial freedom.

Conclusion

Thanks for making it through to the end of this book. I hope it was informative and able to provide you with all of the tools you need to achieve your goals, whatever they may be.

The next step is to apply everything that you have learned and start trading for profit. Being a successful trader takes time, dedication, and commitment. The good news is that it is well within your reach. Kindly take note that the rules in this book are meant to be practiced. You cannot fully understand the meaning of these teachings unless you apply them. Do not be discouraged even if you commit mistakes despite knowing these rules. Again, learning how to trade effectively is just like learning a new skill. It does take time and practice. This is where the power of repetition comes in. Just like with learning any new skill, you will be a better trader the more that you expose yourself to the activities of a trader. However, repetition alone is not enough. You also need to make your own reflections and learn from the experience. Indeed, trading cannot be learned just by reading. You have to experience it and expose yourself to it. This is also the best and only way to find out if you really want to be a professional trader.

Trading can be a very fun activity. In fact, it is not uncommon to find traders who barely notice that they have already spent hours researching a particular market. As a trader, you are responsible for everything and can enjoy being your own boss. Indeed, it is a highly rewarding career. Just like anything that is worth pursuing, it also has its risks. This is why you have these cardinal rules to follow in order to avoid or at least minimize your losses and significantly increase your profits.

There are traders who have left their day jobs and now trade full-time. There are also those who have earned a fortune just by trading in the comfort of their home. Indeed, this is a rewarding career despite its challenges. After all, there is nothing that is worth pursuing without assuming any risks. If you want to be a successful trader, then you need to give yourself a chance to face challenges and be outside of your comfort zone, for this is how you will learn. Last but not least, if you want to be successful, then you should give it your best without reservations.

Finally, if you found this book useful in any way, a review on Amazon is always appreciated!

www.ingramcontent.com/pod-product-compliance
Lightning Source LLC
Chambersburg PA
CBHW071150220526
45468CB00003B/1011